Merry Christmas 2016'
Thanks for your friendship.
Love, Lori

As *Sisters*
IN *Zion*

DEBBIE J. CHI

DESERET
BOOK

Salt Lake City, Utah

Deseret Book is a registered trademark of Deseret Book Company.

Visit us at DeseretBook.com

First printing in hardbound 2012
First printing in paperbound 2016

Library of Congress Cataloging-in-Publication Data

Christensen, Debbie J., author.
  As sisters in Zion / Debbie J. Christensen.
    pages cm
  Summary: "British converts and sisters Emily and Julia Hill, assigned to the Willie handcart company, accompany newly widowed Martha Campkin and her five children to Zion. Emily later pens a poem about her experiences that becomes a cherished song of the LDS Relief Society, 'As Sisters in Zion.'"—Provided by publisher.
  Includes bibliographical references.
  ISBN 978-1-60908-895-8 (hardbound : alk. paper)
  ISBN 978-1-62972-218-4 (paperbound)
  1. Woodmansee, Emily H. (Emily Hill), 1836–1906.   2. Ivins, Julia Hill, 1833–1895.
3. Young, Martha Webb Campkin, 1820–1898.   4. Mormon pioneers—Biography.
5. Mormon women—Biography.   6. Mormon handcart companies.   I. Title.
  BX8693.C47 2012
  289.3092'52—dc23   2011032601

Printed in the United States of America
Alexander's Print Advantage, Lindon, UT

10   9   8   7   6   5   4   3

TO MY "SISTERS"
JULIA, EMILY, AND MARTHA

AND TO ALLISON, HEATHER, ROBIN, CHRIS,
LANA, MARILEE, AND CHRISTINE

As ye are desirous to come into the fold of God, and to be called his people, and are willing to bear one another's burdens, that they may be light; Yea, and are willing to mourn with those that mourn; Yea, and comfort those that stand in need of comfort . . .

Mosiah 18:8–9

Contents

Contents

Acknowledgments

I owe deep gratitude to one man and to many strong, virtuous women. It is interesting that a book on sisters was begun because of my husband, Craig. He was the one who initially found their story and who encouraged me to research it and write about it.

I would also like to acknowledge the sisters in my family. Their goodness and example to all who are fortunate enough to cross their paths are an inspiration to me.

Several other good women I would like to acknowledge include Wendy, Sheri, Jana, the Deseret Book publishing team of Leslie, Tonya, and Heather, and my good friends, Jackie and Meagan—all who made this book possible.

But above all, I am truly grateful to the sisters, Julia and Emily, who have become dear friends to me throughout this journey.

CHAPTER ONE

"As Sisters in Zion"

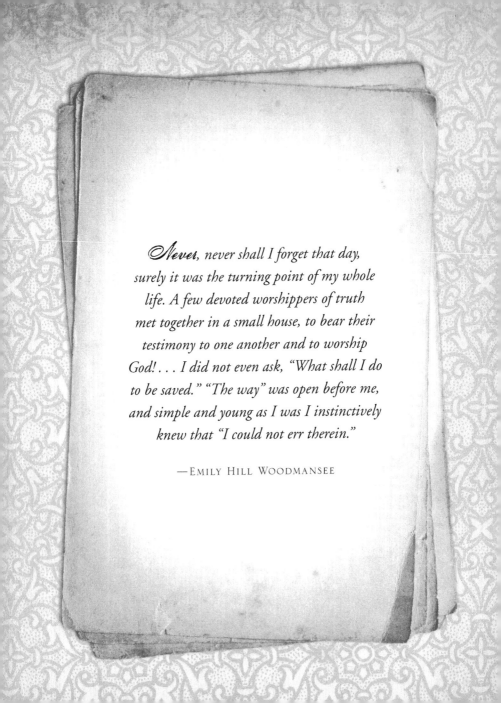

Never, never shall I forget that day, surely it was the turning point of my whole life. A few devoted worshippers of truth met together in a small house, to bear their testimony to one another and to worship God! . . . I did not even ask, "What shall I do to be saved." "The way" was open before me, and simple and young as I was I instinctively knew that "I could not err therein."

—EMILY HILL WOODMANSEE

*I*n the small town of Warminster, Wiltshire, in southern England, in 1848, there lived a young woman named Emily Hill. Only twelve years old, she was a strong, bright, and creative girl who loved to write poems and study in the family Bible. Even at that young age, she was concerned about her eternal salvation and searched the scriptures. She studied the lives of the ancient prophets, especially Isaiah, and wondered why God didn't speak to man anymore.[1]

One day, a cousin, Miriam Slade, came to visit the Hill family. Miriam was a member of The Church of Jesus Christ of Latter-day Saints, and she told the family about the Church, saying that God had spoken from the heavens to a man named Joseph Smith. She invited the Hill family to attend a meeting the following Sunday.

Emily's older sisters laughed and said, "Send Em, she will tell us all about it."[2]

The following Sunday, Emily sat enthralled at the message from the missionaries who were preaching, and she instantly recognized that they were talking about the same church that had been established in the days of the Savior Jesus Christ. Emily recollected: "It was indeed as though I had been brought 'out of darkness into marvelous light,' and I could not shut my eyes against it."[3]

Of the meeting, Emily wrote, "Never, never shall I forget that day, surely it was the turning point of my whole life. A few devoted worshippers of truth met together in a small house, to bear their testimony to one another and to worship God! And He was in their midst and that to bless them. . . . I did not even ask, 'What shall I do to be saved.' 'The way' was open before me, and simple and young as I was I instinctively knew that 'I could not err therein.'"[4]

Thomas Hill, Emily's father, was a wealthy landowner and farmer, and his children were well-educated. He and Elizabeth Slade Hill were the parents of eleven children: Mary Ann (born 1823), Jane (born 1825), Alban (born 1828), Ephraim (born 1830), Charlotte (born 1832), Julia (born January 15, 1833), Frank (born 1834), Emily (born March 24, 1836), twins Esau and Jacob (born 1839, died in infancy), and George (born 1841, died in infancy). Since the three youngest boys had all died in infancy, at the age of five, Emily became the doted-upon youngest living child.

The parents had their own strongly held religious beliefs based in the Wesleyan faith and didn't welcome the message that their daughter brought home from the missionaries. The reverends in the area pressured young Emily, saying that she "wasn't old enough to know [her] own mind, and was altogether too young to judge of so grave a matter."[5] But Emily and her older sister, Julia, were convinced that truth had been restored, and they wanted the missionaries to baptize them. After hearing a powerful testimony of Joseph Smith, Julia exclaimed, "If ever there was a man of God I'm sure he [Joseph] is one, and I'll be a Latter-Day Saint, too!"[6]

Their strict, Victorian-age parents forbade the girls to join up with the Mormons, "a sect that was everywhere spoken against."[7] To ensure the girls wouldn't be further influenced by the missionaries, the parents had the girls watched closely by their older siblings. However, before the missionaries went away, they brought by a member named John Halliday, who bore strong testimony to the girls and gave young Emily a priesthood blessing—a blessing that would not be fulfilled until many years later. In this blessing, Emily was told that if she would remain faithful to her testimony of Jesus Christ throughout her life, she would "write in prose and in verse and thereby comfort the hearts of thousands."[8] That such a promise would be made to an obscure young woman from a small town in England was remarkable, particularly as her involvement in the Church was so severely restricted at that time.

The sisters continued to live with their family for the next four years, until 1852, when they determined to join The Church of Jesus Christ of Latter-day Saints. Emily, then sixteen years of age, had a deep and burning testimony of the Restoration, and Julia, nineteen years old and of a quieter nature, held an equally strong conviction. But that didn't make their sacrifice any easier. The sisters clearly understood that the decision to join the Church meant giving up the comforts of their home, the love of their parents, the warmth of their large family circle, and whatever security they had known as daughters of Thomas and Elizabeth Hill. They were baptized on March 25, 1852.

This act of defiance resulted in their being disowned by their parents and rejected by their entire close-knit family. The loving relationship the girls had previously had with their mother, Elizabeth, was now unequivocally torn apart. Julia, who was particularly close to her younger brother, Frank, was devastated by the family's extreme reaction to their choice.

Emily, a headstrong young woman, respected and honored her equally strong-minded father, but she often butted heads with him. Even so, she idolized her father, and everyone said she bore a close physical resemblance to him. She referred to him as a "man of men" and "my own dear Sire."[9] Her later writings express her lifelong feelings about the alienation she and Julia experienced at the time of their conversion:

> *Oh! this has been one bitter cup*
> *Of many, I have had to drain.*[10]

Throughout her life, Emily carried no hard feelings toward her father and mother and sought often to communicate with them. Of her father, she was to later write:

> *Dear Father, oft my heart is thrill'd*
> *With longing till with pain 'tis sore*
> *Would that my wish could be fulfill'd*
> *That we could meet on earth once more.*[11]

Her thoughts on her mother were also expressed in verse:

> *My Mother's worth, my Mother's love,*
> *Ne'er amplified can be;*
> *Where e'er in retrospect I turn*
> *She is all dear to me.*[12]

Following their baptisms in 1852, and now unwelcome in their parents' home, Julia and Emily decided to gather with the Saints in Zion, in America. The girls took an apprenticeship to a milliner in the neighboring town of Northampton and for four years saved the money that would finance their passage to America and the arduous trek west to the Rocky Mountains. During that time they enjoyed a fond association with the English Saints, who warmly befriended them. Emily said of this time: "There for the first time I enjoyed religious freedom and there also I took my lessons of hard times; preparing me for greater hardships in store."[13]

Finally, in the spring of 1856, the sisters traveled to Liverpool with their fellow Saints. There, at three o'clock A.M. on Sunday, May 4, they embarked on the ship *Thornton* to sail to America. Elder James Gray Willie, who had been preaching in England, was appointed by President Franklin D. Richards as the captain of the company. There were more than 760 Saints on board the ship; most were from England and Scotland, but more than 160 had traveled from Denmark and Sweden to join them.[14]

The sisters stood together on the deck of the ship as it was tugged out from the Bramley-Moore docks in Liverpool. As the ship moved in the dark down the River Mersey and eventually out to sea and the green English countryside receded into the distance, the young women knew they were leaving behind all they had known and loved—their parents and family, their home, their native England—all for their testimonies of the restored gospel. As they contemplated with excitement the adventure before them, they surrendered briefly to heartache and tears. Yet they remained steadfast and confident that what they were doing was right, and their strong testimonies drove them forward in hope and knowledge.

The normal trials of a sea voyage ensued. Since the captain took the ship across the northern route, sightings of giant icebergs were common, and rough waters and storms were frequent. A fire in the passengers' galley one day caused a bit of alarm, but it was quickly extinguished. The sisters were well-liked by the other passengers, and Emily was one of the few attendees of the shipboard wedding of Allen Findlay and Jessie Ireland in the captain's cabin.[15] In all, the group experienced three births, seven deaths, and two marriages over the course of the forty-one day journey at sea.[16]

Their ship's captain was a kindly man named Captain Charles Collins who treated his Latter-day Saint voyagers well during the six-week passage over the Atlantic. He must have been pleased to do so because at the conclusion of the ocean voyage, he wrote a letter to James Willie in which he said that "they are the finest body of emigrants I have ever had the pleasure to convey across the Atlantic—they have always been willing to do and act according to my wish, expressed by myself through you [Willie], and to render me any assistance that I have required from time to time."[17]

Elder James Willie, who appreciated the treatment he and his party received during the crossing, observed: "I felt all the time and still feel to say 'God bless Captain Collins.'"[18] Many of the journals kept of the trip note the kind attention Captain Collins and the ship's doctor gave to the sick and weak.

After six weeks at sea, the *Thornton* arrived safely at the immigration center of Castle Gardens on Manhattan Island in New York City on June 14, 1856. The company was heartily greeted by Elder John Taylor, and also by several gentlemen of the press, who wrote articles for local newspapers, praising "the general appearance and demeanor of the entire Company."[19]

On Tuesday, June 17, the company traveled by rail through Dunkirk, New York. After traveling by steamboat across Lake Erie, they again boarded a train in Toledo, Ohio, where they encountered some unkind railway authorities who didn't like the Mormons and caused them "every inconvenience in their power."[20] Despite that episode, the group continued without further incident on to Chicago.

Up to this point in their journey, there had always been food to eat, but on June 23 the Saints were delayed at a place called Pond Creek where they "had much difficulty in obtaining provisions."[21] Here, the railway bridge across the Mississippi had collapsed, forcing the company to spend another night on the train before taking a ferry across the river. Finally, on June 26, the Saints again boarded a train and took the rails into Iowa City, Iowa, where they were greeted by Elder Daniel Spencer, who had served in England as a counselor to Franklin D. Richards in the mission presidency.

Emily and Julia stayed with the other Saints in a camp just

outside Iowa City until July 15. During this three-week period, the men were employed making yokes and handcarts, and the women, including Julia and Emily, were kept busy sewing tents for the journey—a task made far less pleasant by frequent soaking rains.

With a severe shortage of tents and daily thunderstorms accompanied by raging winds, their accommodations were often primitive and uncomfortable. Most of the Saints in this company had no experience with pioneer life. They did not know how to pitch a tent, build a campfire, or cook outdoors. They were also highly unaccustomed to the typical early summer Midwestern heat and humidity and the notorious Iowa mud created by the frequent deluges of rain.

These enthusiastic Saints from England, Scotland, and Scandinavia were also not fully prepared for the trials and travails of pulling and pushing a handcart over the miles of rough trails that were ahead. Coming from a relatively level elevation and the seemingly benign, gentle landscapes of their home countries, they could simply not envision the ordeal of travel that they were about to face.

Reflecting on the reality of traveling by handcart, Emily, still a proper Victorian young woman and not yet a full-fledged pioneer, wrote: "Yet, for the potent reason that no other way seemed open, and on the principle of 'descending below all things,' I made up my mind to pull a hand cart. 'All the way to Zion,' a foot journey from Iowa to Utah, and pull our luggage, think of it! . . .

The flesh certainly was weak but the spirit was willing, [and] I set down my foot that I would try."[22] Her bravado may have been naïve, but she and her sister Julia soon had ample opportunity to demonstrate their pluck. It began when they met a woman named Martha Campkin.

CHAPTER TWO

"We'll All Work Together"

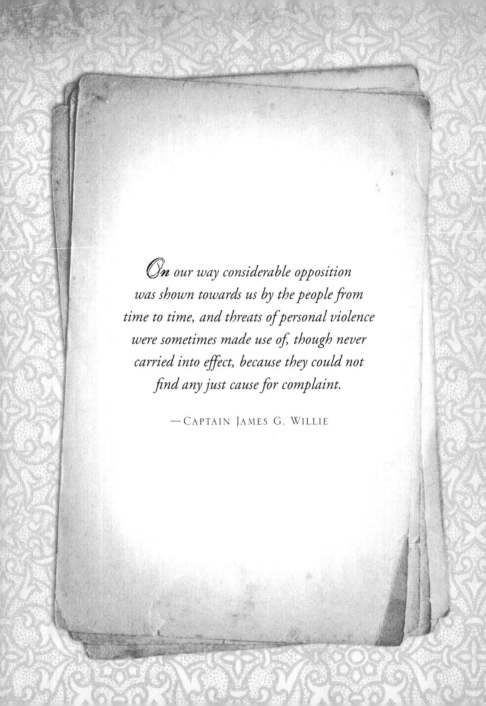

*On our way considerable opposition
was shown towards us by the people from
time to time, and threats of personal violence
were sometimes made use of, though never
carried into effect, because they could not
find any just cause for complaint.*

—Captain James G. Willie

*I*saac Campkin, a successful boot and shoemaker of Biggles-
wade, Bedfordshire, England, and his wife, Martha Webb
Campkin, were baptized members of the Church in November
1850. Martha was described as a "quiet, dressy little woman" and
Isaac was known to be an eloquent, "genial, tall, good looking
man."[1]

Together Isaac and Martha had six children: Wilford George
(born 1847), Rebecca (born 1849, but who died of diptheria at the
age of three), Francessa (born 1850), Harriet (born 1852), Martha
Ann (born 1854), and James Isaac (born 1855).

Shortly before the birth of James Isaac, Isaac began prepara-
tions for the voyage to America and the journey to join the Saints
in Salt Lake City. He sold his business and his home. A missionary
serving in the area asked for a loan of six hundred dollars to help

some other families immigrate and promised to return that money to the Campkin family in New York so they could purchase oxen, a wagon, and supplies for their journey west to Zion.

The Campkins embarked from Liverpool with their five young children on the ship *Caravan* in February 1856. The 454 Saints on board were under the care and direction of Daniel Tyler.[2] They arrived in New York on March 27, 1856. Neither the money nor the missionary awaited them.

Since the European Saints were gathering in St. Louis, Missouri, to travel west together, the Campkins took a train to St. Louis. In England, Isaac had been ill with smallpox and had not felt well since, but after arriving in St. Louis, he developed a severe cold which quickly became pneumonia. He died unexpectedly three days later at the age of thirty-three.

Isaac may have been planning to set up a shoe store in St. Louis to replenish his funds so he and his family could travel to Zion, but now Martha was suddenly left a widow with five children under eight years of age. And a poor widow at that. She had no wagon or supplies and no possible means of getting herself and her children to Zion. Her friends encouraged her to wait a season.

Determined to fulfill Isaac's dream of his family reaching Zion, Martha pressed forward and the bereaved little family found its way to Iowa City a few months later. There Martha spoke with Captain James Willie about her traveling west with his handcart company. He discouraged her immediately, pointing out that she couldn't pull a handcart alone and that it would be useless for her to think of doing so.

It was then that the Widow Campkin met Emily and Julia Hill, who were also traveling by themselves. The sisters offered to help pull the cart and tend the children, and the heaven-sent partnership was formed. With the offer of two strong, believing young women to help pull the handcart, Captain Willie relented and agreed to let Martha Campkin and her young children go with the company.

What a unique partnership of sisters this became. To Martha, who had been mourning the sudden loss of her husband and attempting to simply survive and help her children to do the same, it was an answer to prayer—having these two eager and willing, physically strong young women come to her assistance. She now had help keeping her little family organized and moving along the trail with the rest of the company, to say nothing of the aid they would be in pulling the handcart and cooking the meals. By sharing the duties with her two new friends, the impossible became possible.

Julia and Emily also benefited from the newfound association with Sister Campkin and her children. Although they had grown up in a large family, the three youngest brothers of Julia and Emily had died as infants. Missing their brothers and the rest of their beloved family, the girls soon bonded with the youngsters of the Campkin clan. They also became fast friends with Martha, and reveled in learning from her and her children.

Years later, one of Martha's granddaughters, Ida Young Thorne, wrote fondly of Julia and Emily Hill helping Martha pull the handcart and tend the family. Martha's oldest daughter, Francessa, also recalled in her journal that Emily, a "poetess," was very kind to the family, and that the sisters' kindness would never be forgotten by the Campkin family.[3]

The three women and five children were also assisted along the way by a young man named Thomas Young.

Thomas had joined the Church as a young man in England and had gathered with the Saints to sail on the *Caravan,* the same ship as the Campkins. He became acquainted with the Campkin family on the ship and traveled with them by train to St. Louis. When Isaac's health began to fail, Isaac asked Thomas if he would care for the family, and Thomas promised that he would. Thomas secured a job as a teamster for the Abraham Smoot wagon company, which joined with the Willie handcart company. Thomas befriended the little troupe of women and children and traveled the trail at the same time as the fourth handcart company (the Willie company), although sometimes on the opposite side of the river.[4]

Julia and Emily Hill and Martha Campkin and her children

were assigned to Levi Savage's group of one hundred Saints, with Brother Savage also being the captain of the Perpetual Emigration Fund (PEF) wagons that accompanied the handcarts. Campkin family journals note that the older children walked most of the way, with Sister Campkin riding in a wagon only occasionally to care for the baby.[5] The Willie company included "nearly 500 people, 120 handcarts, 25 tents (each sleeping 20 people), 5 supply wagons (carrying food and tents), 24 oxen (for pulling 4 of the wagons), 5 mules (4 were used to pull the other wagon), and 45 beef cattle and milk cows."[6]

Women and children traveling alone were never assigned to tents that men occupied, so the Campkins and the Hills were most likely assigned the same tent. A typical evening scene would usually involve Julia and Emily helping Martha feed the exhausted children and get them settled down for the evening. The women would then bake the bread the group would eat the next day. The ration of flour for the trek across Iowa was meager—ten ounces per person—but they were able to supplement that with wild game, meat from the cattle, and other supplies, most supplied by fellow pioneers with the means to procure the additional food.

Evenings were also the time to make needed repairs to their equipment, which had been bounced and jostled on the rough trail throughout the day. Since most of the handcarts in the Willie company had been made from unseasoned wood, getting the handcarts ready each night for the next day's travel became a burdensome chore, for men and women alike. A deep and long-lasting friendship was built between this widowed mother and the two single sisters as they worked side by side in the enormous task they had taken on.

At the beginning of their journey, the Willie company was making good time. The Saints were strong in their resolve to get to Zion and with 1,300 miles of travel ahead, they were moving well and averaging fifteen miles a day. However, they encountered some opposition along their way in the early stages of their march. Captain Willie reported, "On our way considerable opposition was shown towards us by the people [of Iowa] from time to time, and threats of personal violence were sometimes made use of, though never carried into effect, because they could not find any just cause for complaint."[7]

On Sunday, July 20, Captain Willie and the other leaders preached to the Saints and filled the camp with the Spirit of heaven, but the following Monday night a mob of angry men surrounded the camp, swearing and cursing at the Mormons. The Saints doubled their guards, and the hostile men left without further incident, though tensions remained high.

Five days later, on July 25, while camped at Muddy Creek, a group of men came with a warrant to "search the bottoms of our wagons for young women, who, as were alleged, were tied down there with ropes."[8] They found nothing amiss and left.

While passing through these frontier towns, Julia and Emily also received mysterious, anonymous notes "setting forth the hardships and impossibilities of such a journey, and offering [them] inducements to stay."[9] Though the motives of the anonymous writers may have been sinister, it is true that a handcart pulled entirely by young women in that Victorian era would have been shocking. Public opinion being what it was in those days, many assumed the worst of the Mormons. Whatever the motive of the writers, the invitations were always disregarded, for the sisters paid them no heed.

The handcart company's experiences with those not of the Mormon faith were not always bad. A memorable and welcome event happened on July 31. As the company passed through Des Moines, Iowa, a generous man, Mr. Charles Good, kindly presented Captain Willie with fifteen pairs of well-made children's boots.[10] The entire company asked that "Good Charles Good," as they called him, be blessed for his kindness. Perhaps some of Martha's children were the grateful recipients of a pair of those precious and probably life-saving boots.

Despite voiced concerns about the lateness of the season, on

Saturday, August 16, part of the fourth handcart company, including the little band of sisters, pulled out from Florence, Nebraska, under the direction of Captain Willie. They were accompanied by eleven wagons, including Levi Savage's Perpetual Emigration Fund wagons and some independently owned wagons. They journeyed a short distance to Little Pappea where they camped with Colonel Almon Babbitt and four of his wagons. The following day, August 17, the remainder of the wagons and carts under Captain Willie arrived, and the company spent time making needed repairs to their handcarts and tents before continuing on their journey.

As the sisters and others in the pioneer company walked through fields of sunflowers or expanses of tall prairie grasses on the plains, it was not always a joyous, peaceful trek through a beautiful countryside. Thunderstorms would occasionally form, the heavens would open, and the Saints would be poured upon. To escape the torrential downpours, which could appear swiftly and leave just as quickly, sometimes the Saints would hunker down under the handcarts or under one of the wagons traveling with them, especially if there was thunder and lightning. With no other shelter near, children would huddle next to their mothers and whimper and cry as lightning tore through the sky accompanied by ominous booms of thunder. Other times, the group would simply trudge on through the dark and foreboding storms. Following the cloudbursts, the completely soaked Saints would spread their drenched belongings and wet clothes over the handcarts to dry as they moved forward.

These Saints were used to the gentle rains, green hills, and majestic forests or to the noise and bustle of city life in their native countries, but this raw display of nature's power was completely different. The immensity of the sky, the limitless horizon, the moaning of the wind, and the total lack of comfort or shelter was often overwhelming to the senses. The constant need to push or pull the cart; the unrelenting heat or cold, hunger, and thirst; and the numbing exhaustion that were their constant companions made the journey at times seem unending and the destination unreachable.

And yet they persevered.

CHAPTER THREE

"The Blessings of God on Our Labors We'll Seek"

Oh! little we knew of our troubles in store,
Of the wilderness vast, that we had to pass o'er.
And sometimes I think the provisions most wise
That troubles ahead are oft hid from our eyes
Unless our foreknowledge the evil could cure
'Tis best not to know all we have to endure.

—EMILY HILL WOODMANSEE

*B*y September, the company had reached the eastern slopes of the Rocky Mountains. As they gazed up at the massive purple heights above them, Emily and Julia shivered with dread at what was going to be required. It was fall; the leaves were changing, and the nights were cold. John Chislett, who was a subcaptain over one hundred in the company and who had previously traveled in the Rockies, said: "The mountains [were] before us, [and] as we approached nearer to them, [they] revealed themselves to view mantled nearly to their base in snow, and tokens of a coming storm were discernible in the clouds which each day seemed to lower around us."[1]

The sisters were now pulling their cart up the foothills through soft, sandy footing. The wheels would drag through the loose soil, and it became more and more a necessity to push the handcart than to pull. In addition, apprehension about possible Indian attacks had spread throughout the group. On August 29, they came upon a camp of friendly Omaha Indians who sold buffalo meat to the company. "These Indians informed us of a murder, which had been committed on the 25th [of August] by the Cheyennes, on two of Col. Babbitt's men and a Mrs. Wilson and her child. We subsequently passed by the scene of the murder and covered up the graves."[2]

This experience was unnerving to the entire company, but especially to those women who were the sole protectors for their families. The attack occurred just nine days after they had camped with Colonel Babbitt, a member of the Nauvoo Legion, at Little Pappea. Colonel Babbitt survived the ambush by the Cheyenne, but he himself was killed by them three weeks later at Fort Laramie.[3]

Captain Willie expressed additional concern in his journal, noting: "On the morning of Thursday, 4th Sept. (being 265 miles west of Florence) we found that 30 of our oxen were missing. We stayed to search for them till the 6 and during our stay Col. Babbitt came up and reported that the Cheyennes had attacked a small Californian train and killed a woman."[4] In retaliation, the U.S. marshalls killed thirteen Cheyenne and confiscated their horses. This put the fourth handcart company right in the middle of the trouble. Emily, Julia, and Martha were constantly concerned and ever alert. The season was advancing, the weather was getting colder, thirty oxen and cattle were gone—possibly from a stampede—and the Cheyenne were unpredictable. A terrible storm at this time had washed away any hoofprints the thirty cattle had made, so the men were unable to follow their tracks and never located any of the missing animals, adding another element of difficulty to their journey.

On Sunday, September 7, Captain Willie spoke to the concerned company and said, "The whole strength of the camp, that of men, women, children, and beasts, must be applied under the direction of the officers of the camp for the one object in view, the early resumption and speedy & final completion of the journey."[5]

As the cold nights and the gravity of these trials settled upon the Saints, the little band of sisters intensified their resolve to get to the Valley. Their prayers and petitions to God became more fervent and specific as they contemplated the storms and mountains that lay between them and the Zion they sought. Awed by the immensity and ruggedness of the Rocky Mountains, with each step increasing in height and ominous danger and each mountain a foreshadow of the granite monster behind it, this was a time that their testimonies were tempered in the fire of adversity. The sisters were sustained in response to their powerful pleadings to see the city of Saints with their mortal eyes.[6]

The burning desire of Emily, Julia, and Martha to get to the

Valley kept them moving through the storms and trials. They had learned they needed each other. Alone they might have failed, but together they hoped they could succeed and live. But there was still much to be endured.

Because of extremely unfortunate miscommunication in instructions to the supply wagons sent out from Salt Lake City to help the handcart companies, no supply wagons had yet gone far enough to reach the Willie company. When relief wagons were sent from Salt Lake City in response to President Brigham Young's plea on October 4 to bring these Saints in from the plains, those rescuers actually met supply wagons returning to the Valley, still full of flour and other life-sustaining goods.

By October 19, the Saints in the fourth handcart company had exhausted all their resources; that day the last ration of flour was issued. Their strength was depleted, and many saw death on the plains as an absolute certainty. Julia, who had struggled throughout the journey, was in true peril.

In the early afternoon a fierce wind began and the first winter snow began to fall. It was at that moment that an advance party from the relief wagons from Salt Lake City arrived. Stephen Taylor, Joseph A. Young, Cyrus Wheelock, and Abel Garr had been sent ahead of the relief wagons to find the handcart companies still on the plains and let them know more help was on the way. Many in the handcart company had already died of exposure and exhaustion, and the pitiful survivors of the Willie company were camped next to the frozen Sweetwater River, surrounded by a sea of swirling snow, and fainting because of hunger and fatigue. The pioneers had given all they could give when shouts rang out in the evening, "The rescuers have come!"

But the end was not yet in sight. In order to travel so quickly, this small group of rescuers in a light wagon did not have an abundance of provisions with them. They brought with them a little flour, some onions, and hope. Then they were on their way, as they had been charged, to find the Martin handcart company.

Joseph A. Young, one of the rescuers, had served a mission to England and recognized Emily. Appalled at her condition, he gave her a small onion. Emily did not eat it immediately but carried it away. Later that night she came upon a seriously ill man lying close to a fire. Emily gave him the onion, and he later said that this act of kindness saved his life.[7]

Joy flooded the souls of the handcart company in the realization that God had not forgotten them. Relief had been sent to succor and comfort those who would have otherwise surely perished on the desolate, snow-covered, high plains of Wyoming.

Reflecting on their suffering during this part of their journey to Zion, Emily wrote a poem about her experience. A portion of it follows:

Hunger and Cold

*A reminiscence of life on the plains
with a Handcart Company*

Oh! little we knew of our troubles in store,
Of the wilderness vast, that we had to pass o'er.
And sometimes I think the provisions most wise
That troubles ahead are oft hid from our eyes
Unless our foreknowledge the evil could cure
'Tis best not to know all we have to endure.

Each day (save the Sabbath) we journeyed with care
Looking out for the redmen who lurked in their lair.
Folks not of our party, who with us had been
The Indians had murdered, their graves we had seen. . . .

At length came the climax—how well I remember
That cold, dismal night in the month of November.
Faint and fasting, we camped by a hard frozen stream
Here nothing we had, but of plenty could dream.

Our rations eked out with discretion and care,
Had utterly vanished, "the cupboard was bare."
Not a morsel to eat could we anywhere see,
Cold, weary and hungry and helpless were we.

Our woes were pathetic and everywhere round
Every inch of the prairie was snow covered ground,
Shut off from the world as in ocean's mid waves,
The desolate plains offer nothing but graves.
Death seemed but a question of limited time,
Yet the faith of these faint ones was truly sublime!
On the brink of the tomb few succumbed to despair,
Our trust was in God, and our strength was in prayer.

Oh, whence came those shouts in the still, starry night,
That thrilled us and filled us with hope and delight?
The cheers of new comers, a jubilant sound
Of triumph and joy over precious ones found.
Life, Life was the treasure held out to our view,
By the "Boys from the Valley," so brave and so true,
The "Boys from the Valley," sent out by their chief,
Brought clothing and food and abundant relief.

O'er mountainous steeps, over drearisome plains
They sought us, and found us, thank God for their pains!

Hurrah! and hurrah! from the feeble and strong.
Hurrah! and hurrah! loud the echoes prolong.
They were saviors, these men whom we hardly had seen,
Yet it seemed that for ages, acquainted we'd been.

When Fate introduces Compassion to Need,
Friendships quickly are founded and ripen with speed.
Weatherworn were our friends, but like kings in disguise
Their souls' native grandeur shone out of their eyes.

Oh, soft were their hearts who with courage like steel,
Left their homes in the Valley our sorrow to heal. . . .

For helpful and kind, as a woman or Saint,
These men cheered the feeble, the frozen and faint.
God bless them for heroes, the tender and bold,
Who rescued our remnant from hunger and cold. . . .

Ups and downs are our fate; for the best 'tis I ween,
Some woes we forget as though ne'er they had been,
But while memory her hold of my being retains
I'll remember the lesson I learned on the plains.
If fortune withholds what I deem would be good,
I try to be thankful for shelter and food.
If disposed e'er to murmur, the wish is controlled,
When I think of that season of hunger and cold.[8]

CHAPTER FOUR

"With Earnest Endeavor"

We buried our dead, got up our teams, and about 9 o'clock A.M. commenced ascending the Rocky Ridge. This was a severe day. The wind blew awful hard and cold. The ascent was some five miles long and some places steep and covered with deep snow. We became weary, sat down to rest, and some became chilled and commenced to freeze.

—LEVI SAVAGE

*S*now continued to fall for the next few days, and it became evident that the relief wagons full of food, bedding, and clothing were waiting out the storm somewhere fairly close at hand. Captain Willie and Joseph Elder left the Saints at the Sixth Crossing of the Sweetwater to try and find the wagons and apprise the leaders of the destitute situation of the Saints by the Sweetwater.

Three days after their departure, the two men returned. They were followed closely by several covered wagons, each pulled by four horses.

As John Chislett recalled:

> The news ran through the camp like wildfire, and all who were able to leave their beds turned out *en masse* to see them. . . . Shouts of joy rent the air; strong men wept

till tears ran freely down their furrowed and sun-burnt cheeks, and little children partook of the joy which some of them hardly understood, and fairly danced around with gladness. . . . The brethren were so overcome that they could not for some time utter a word.[1]

Chislett was put in charge of the distribution of food and clothing and bedding, and reported:

> That evening, for the first time in quite a period, the songs of Zion were to be heard in the camp, and peals of laughter issued from the little knots of people as they chatted around the fires. The change seemed almost miraculous, so sudden was it from grave to gay, from sorrow to gladness, from mourning to rejoicing. With the cravings of hunger satisfied, and with hearts filled with gratitude to God and our good brethren, we all united in prayer, and then retired to rest.[2]

It was October 23, 1856, and the ascent of Rocky Ridge—the Gethsemane of their sacrifice—was still ahead.

Rocky Ridge is known as the place where many members of the Willie company met their Maker. Although sixteen relief wagons had reached them by now, ten of the wagons continued on their way to try and find the Martin handcart company, known to be at least a week behind the Willie company. Only six relief wagons stayed with the Willie company, not nearly enough to help all those who needed assistance getting up the ridge. The weakest of the Saints were placed in the wagons, but most members of the handcart company still needed to pull their own handcarts through the snow to the top of the ridge.

John Chislett described how it was accomplished:

> By all hands getting to one cart we could travel; so we moved one of the carts a few rods, and then went back and brought up the other. After moving in this way for a while, we overtook other carts at different points of the hill, until we had six carts, not one of which could be moved by the parties owning it.
>
> I put our collective strength to three carts at a time, took them a short distance, and then brought up the other three. Then by travelling over the hill three times—twice forward and once back—I succeeded after hours of toil in bringing my little company to the summit.[3]

Levi Savage wrote in his journal of the harrowing day that the Willie company ascended Rocky Ridge:

We buried our dead, got up our teams, and about 9 o'clock A.M. commenced ascending the Rocky Ridge. This was a severe day. The wind blew awful hard and cold. The ascent was some five miles long and some places steep and covered with deep snow. We became weary, sat down to rest, and some became chilled and commenced to freeze. Brothers Atwood, Woodward, and myself remained with the teams, they being perfectly loaded down with the sick and children, so thickly stacked I was fearful some would smother.[4]

Julia was not as physically strong as her sister and, earlier in the journey when her health had given out, she had occasionally ridden in the handcart. By Rocky Ridge, Julia was in serious trouble. A family journal states that "Julia, worn out by the rigors of the journey, had all but succumbed to the onslaught of storm and exposure."[5] When Julia collapsed near the summit of Rocky Ridge, her face gray and her eyes lifeless, Emily stopped her handcart and came to her sister. She bent down and tenderly lifted Julia from the snow and helped her to the handcart. Together they moved forward to a camp at Rock Creek Hollow to survive yet another day. Martha and all of her children also made it to Rock Creek safely.

By all accounts, it took Levi Savage, John Chislett, Millen Atwood, William Woodward, and several others until dawn the next day to get all of the Saints to the camp at Rock Creek Hollow.

Fifteen pioneers were buried that day, thirteen of them in a common grave.

Over the next ten days, the Saints pulled their handcarts to Fort Bridger, with more Saints perishing along the way. They continued to meet with rescue wagons, and although a few stayed with them, most of the relief wagons proceeded on to aid the Martin handcart company.

CHAPTER FIVE

"The Errand of Angels"

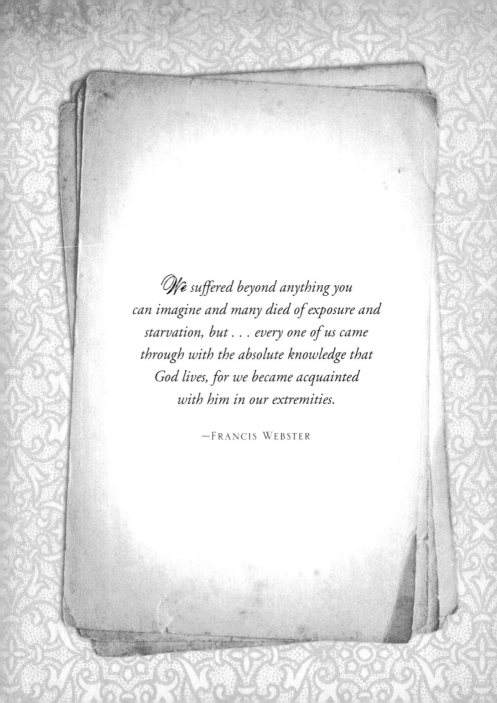

We suffered beyond anything you can imagine and many died of exposure and starvation, but . . . every one of us came through with the absolute knowledge that God lives, for we became acquainted with him in our extremities.

—Francis Webster

Having survived the long crossing and the indescribable suffering caused by the early Wyoming winter, and with the help of those who had been sent, the Willie handcart company arrived in the Salt Lake Valley on 9 November 1856, descending into the Valley through Emigration Canyon in four feet of snow. President Brigham Young directed that the exhausted people be taken into homes and nursed back to health over the winter.

On Sunday, 16 November 1856, a week after the Willie company entered the Salt Lake Valley, President Brigham Young stood in the Tabernacle and spoke to the people. In his speech, he addressed the suffering of the Willie and Martin handcart companies:

> I rise to make a few remarks, to satisfy the feelings
> of the people and correct their minds and judgment. . . .

When we have done all we can, then the Lord is under obligation, and will not disappoint the faithful; He will perform the rest. . . . But, under the circumstances, it was *our duty* to assist them [the companies]. . . . We had the power and ability to help them, therefore it became our duty to do so.

The Lord was not brought under obligation in the matter, so He had put the means in our possession to render them the assistance they needed.[1]

There ensued some heated discussion among the Saints regarding the tragedy encountered by members of the Willie handcart company. Some were critical of Church leaders for permitting the company to set out for the Salt Lake Valley so late in the season. Brigham Young refuted the criticism with the following reasoning: "If Saints do right and have performed all required of them in this probation, they are under no more obligation, and then it is no matter whether they live or die, for their work here is finished. This is a doctrine I believe."[2] He pointed out as well that the Saints who went out to rescue the survivors and who took them afterward into their homes to be nurtured demonstrated the depth of their own faith and devotion.

Others argued that if the members of the handcart company had not gone out on the trail, they may have perished from want in the frontier communities where they had no shelter and had no reasonable hope of receiving help from the residents because of the anti-Mormon sentiment that was prevalent in those communities. They could not stay and so went on.

But perhaps the most poignant defense of the decision to leave late in the season was made years later by a survivor of the journey, Francis Webster, who had traveled with the Martin handcart company. After listening to criticism and critique of the handcart expedition, he stood up in his Sunday School class and testified:

> I ask you to stop this criticism. You are discussing a matter you know nothing about. Cold historic facts mean nothing here, for they give no proper interpretation of the questions involved. Mistake to send the handcart company out so late in the season? Yes. But I was in that company and my wife was in it. . . . We suffered beyond anything you can imagine and many died of exposure and starvation, but . . . every one of us came through with the absolute knowledge that God lives, for we became acquainted with him in our extremities.
>
> I have pulled my handcart when I was so weak and weary from illness and lack of food that I could hardly put one foot ahead of the other. I have looked ahead and seen a patch of sand or a hill slope and I have said, I can go only that far and there I must give

up, for I cannot pull the load through it. I have gone to that sand, and when I reached it, the cart began pushing me. I have looked back many times to see who was pushing my cart, but my eyes saw no one. I knew then that the angels of God were there.

Was I sorry that I chose to come by handcart? No. Neither then nor any minute of my life since. The price we paid to become acquainted with God was a privilege to pay, and I am thankful that I was privileged to come in the Martin handcart company.[3]

CHAPTER SIX

"Oh, Naught but the Spirit's Divinest Tuition"

Two, of a household band,
Two, in the flush of youth,
Came hither from their home afar,
Led Zionward, by Faith's bright star,
And love of God and Truth.

—EMILY HILL WOODMANSEE

Martha Webb Campkin Young

After Martha Campkin arrived in the Valley, she married Thomas Young—sixteen years her junior—who had promised her dying husband that he would take care of her and make sure that she and the children got safely to Zion. A family story exists that not one of Martha's children lost a finger or toe to frostbite, partly because Thomas Young would rub their hands and feet. In 1860, Martha, Thomas, and her five children settled in Three Mile Creek (now Perry, Utah), where many of their descendants live today. They had three children together.

Martha was an industrious woman; she was known as a good cook and an excellent housekeeper, and she and her daughters braided straw hats as a small business. Family tradition holds that the family also raised produce that they took to the railroad town of Corinne and for which they were paid in gold dust. Known for their hospitality, she and her family permitted travelers to camp on their farmland. Martha was stalwart and faithful to the gospel all the days of her life. She died in Perry, at the age of seventy-eight.[1]

Julia Hill Ivins

One of the rescuers who answered Brigham Young's call to rescue the Saints out on the plains was Israel Ivins. He was one of the few who stayed with the Willie company, while others went in search of the Martin company. He escorted the Willie company all the way to the Valley. In February 1857, three months after her arrival in the Salt Lake Valley, Julia Hill became Israel's second wife, with the approval of his first wife, Anna Lowrie Ivins. Anna had two living children at the time: Caroline, who was twelve, and Anthony, a five-year-old.

Shortly after Israel and Julia were wed, Israel moved his families to the Provo area. He did not want them in the Salt Lake Valley with the approach of Johnston's Army. Returning to Salt Lake the next year proved a hardship to Julia and her newborn son, Israel Junior. Baby Israel died within a month of their return. Ultimately, Julia and Israel had eight children together, four of whom died before the age of two.

Julia's experiences on the Willie trek helped prepare her for these difficult times and also strengthened her for the work she did in helping to settle the Dixie Mission in St. George, Utah.

The families of Julia and Anna lived harmoniously together. Julia took charge of the daily running of the households, while Anna worked in the St. George Temple.[2] The town of Ivins, near St. George, is named after Israel and Anna's son Anthony.

Israel, Anna, Julia, and Julia's son Frank (who died at eight months, but whom she named after her dear brother) are all buried in the old St. George cemetery.

Julia was a virtuous and righteous woman all the days of her life. Her patriarchal blessing says this of her: "He was well pleased . . . when you received the gospel. His angels rejoiced over you at your baptism. . . . You came in with a pure heart and a contrite spirit. You have left your [earthly] Father's home and your friends and have come unto Zion that you might fulfill all the promises of your [Heavenly] Father."[3]

When Julia died unexpectedly at age sixty-three, Emily penned tender lines, entitled "My Sister," in memory of her beloved sister. An excerpt follows:

MY SISTER

In loving remembrance of Julia Hill Ivins,
suddenly called Home, February 14, 1895

Two, of a household band,
Two, in the flush of youth,
Came hither from their home afar,
Led Zionward, by Faith's bright star,
And love of God and Truth.
Boughs from a parent stem,
By sacred kinship wed,
Are parted—One of them
Is left, and One is dead. . . .

Hail, ransomed, cheery soul,
Rescued from earthly bands,
Uplifted from this world of ours,
Thou art at home amid the flowers
That bloom in fairer lands.
Thou art at home indeed
With friends, beloved of yore,

From all affliction freed—
Where vexing cares are o'er.

Restful, the blissful change,
Yet active still thou'lt be,
Thy useful efforts will not cease—
Rather love's labors will increase
And bring more joy to thee.
Expanded is thy scope,
Exalted is thy sphere—
And yet we fondly hope
Thou wilt at times be near. . . .

Life's span is short at best
Precious is time and fleet
Father, assist us, lest we fail,
Assist us, that we may prevail
And all our tasks complete!
Sweet Mercy shuts out none
From bliss, who've bravely striven;
To such is victory given
Through the Atoning One!

Triumphant words—Well done!
For life long toil, Divine amends,
Full compensation, true success

Comprising endless happiness
Shared with delightful friends.
Nevertheless today
In loneliness we bow
Lord, be our present stay
Uphold and cheer us NOW.[4]

Emily Hill Woodmansee

n June 1857, when she was just twenty-two years old, Emily married thirty-five-year-old handcart rescuer William Gill Mills as his second wife. William was a poet in his own right and had written the words to "Arise, O Glorious Zion," found in the 1985 *Hymns of The Church of Jesus Christ of Latter-day Saints*.[5] He and his first wife, Louisa Avelina Sleater, did not have any children. In October 1859, Emily and William had a daughter, whom they named Avelina. William and Emily also adopted nine-year-old Sarah Alexandrina (Alexina) Bray, who had come across the plains in the

1855 Milo Andrus company, and whose mother had passed away in 1859.[6] In 1860, William asked Brigham Young to send him on a mission to England,[7] and Louisa went with him, leaving Emily, Avelina, and Alexina alone in Salt Lake City. Emily provided for herself, Avelina, and Alexina for four years by taking in boarders. At some point, whether in England or back in the states, William was excommunicated and subsequently wrote Emily renouncing polygamy, his marriage to her, and his child.[8]

Of that experience, Emily said: "No one can realize what such an ordeal is, unless they have passed through it. All that I had hitherto suffered seemed like child's play compared to being deserted by the one in whom I had chosen to place the utmost confidence."[9] *History of Utah* states: "But she was a bright and capable business woman, and by her industry succeeded not only in supporting herself [and her children], but in purchasing a home."[10]

In 1864, Emily married Joseph Woodmansee, with whom she had eight additional children, two of whom died as infants. She was his third wife. *History of Utah* gives an additional tribute to her: "Mrs. Woodmansee has seen many reverses, but her innate courage and ability have made her equal to all occasions. Her husband having lost heavily in mining speculations, she again entered upon a business career, and made a phenomenal success in real estate for several years."[11]

In 1869, thirteen years after surviving the hardships of the crossing, Emily penned her feelings about "her sisters in Zion," the women who had helped her and whom she had helped. She titled this ten-verse poem "Song of the Sisters of the Female Relief Society." She originally set the song to the tune "Hail to the Brightness of Zion's Glad Morning."

SONG OF THE SISTERS OF THE FEMALE RELIEF SOCIETY

[Words that are in the current hymn "As Sisters in Zion" are in brackets]

As sisters in Zion, we'll all pull [work] *together,*
The blessings of God on our labors we'll seek;
We'll build up his Kingdom with earnest endeavor;
We'll comfort the weary, and strengthen the weak.

We'll turn from our follies, our pride and our weakness,
The vain, foolish fashions of Babel despise;
We'll seek for the garments of truth and of meekness,
And learn to be useful and happy and wise.

We'll wear what is sensible, neat and becoming
The daughters of Zion—the children of light;
We'll work with a will, while the angels are scanning
Our aims and our actions from morning till night.

We'll bring up our children to be self sustaining;
To love and to do what is noble and right;
When we rest from our labors, these dear ones remaining,
Will bear off the Kingdom and "fight the good fight."

Nor shall our attention be wholly restricted
To training our children or shaping our dress;

The aged, the feeble, and poor and afflicted,
Our labors shall comfort, our efforts shall bless.

"The Lord hath established the cities of Zion,
The poor of his people are trusting in Him."
He makes us a source for His poor to rely on;
Oh! shall we not brighten the eyes that are dim.

Oh! shall we not hasten to soothe the condition
Of the humble, the needy, the honest and pure?
Oh! let us remember, whate'er our amibition—
'Tis our duty, our mission, to comfort the poor.

'Tis the office of Angels, conferred upon woman;
[The errand of angels is given to women,]
And this is a Right that, as woman, we claim;
[And this is a gift that, as sisters, we claim;]
To do whatsoever is gentle and human;
To cheer and to bless in humanity's name.

How vast is our vision; how wondrous our mission,
[How vast is our purpose, how broad is our mission,]
If we but fulfill it in spirit and deed.
Oh, naught but the Spirit's divinest tuition
Can give us the wisdom to truly succeed.

Then, as sisters in Zion, we'll all pull together,
The blessings of God on our labors we'll seek;
We'll build up his Kingdom with earnest endeavor;
We'll comfort the weary, and strengthen the weak.[12]

This poem resided unnoticed in the Church archives for over 116 years, until 1985, when the Hymn Book Executive Committee under the direction of Brother Michael Moody searched for a suitable theme for the sisters of the Relief Society. Emily's poem was located, taken out, and put to music by Janice Kapp Perry. The new hymn, which is to be sung "resolutely," is entitled "As Sisters in Zion" and now serves as something of an anthem for the women of the Church. It is Hymn No. 309 in the 1985 edition of the *Hymns of The Church of Jesus Christ of Latter-day Saints.*

The hymn's inclusion in the hymnal is a direct fulfillment of the promise made to young Emily in the priesthood blessing given to her by Elder John Halliday prior to leaving England that if she would remain faithful to her testimony of Jesus Christ throughout her life, she would influence the world by the thousands through her prose and verse.[13] Perhaps she has influenced millions, not merely thousands, as her song is sung in languages across the world.

Emily was faithful throughout her life to her testimony of Jesus Christ. Her poetry was published in the *Improvement Era,* the *Young Woman's Journal,* and the *Women's Exponent,* and the 1927 LDS Church hymnbook contained eight of her hymns (see pages 73 through 80). She passed away October 6, 1906, at the age of seventy.

CHAPTER SEVEN

"To Cheer and to Bless in Humanity's Name"

'Tis the office of Angels, conferred upon woman;
and this is a Right that, as woman, we claim;
To do whatsoever is gentle and human;
To cheer and to bless in humanity's name.

—EMILY HILL WOODMANSEE

*D*uring a particularly difficult time in my life, when I was seeking comfort and direction through prayer, I had a dream about my great-great-grandmother Julia Hill and her sister Emily.

In my dream, I saw Julia and Emily stranded in the snow near the windy summit of Rocky Ridge in western Wyoming with others in the Willie handcart company. The young women were shivering from the cold, and Julia was sitting down in the snow. It was clear that she had reached the end of her endurance and was unable to go on. Her younger sister, Emily—who was herself freezing—lifted Julia to her feet. Julia began to weep, but no tears came, only soft whimpering sounds. Emily lovingly wrapped her arms around her sister, and together they made their way slowly to their handcart and continued the torturous climb up Rocky Ridge.

I do not know if the dream was an accurate depiction of what they actually experienced, but, to me, that is not important. Certainly the trauma that the members of the Willie and Martin handcart companies experienced was real, as we have learned from so many firsthand journal sources.

What is important is the lesson I learned. I was able to see clearly the parallel between their struggle and the one I was going through. Though what I was struggling to resolve was not as dramatic or as life-threatening as their crisis, I witnessed how the sisters strengthened each other as well as their friend Martha and her children. Their example of courage strengthened me and helped me through my own challenge.

Where did this little band of sisters find the remarkable courage, determination, and strength to make this epic journey and travel through the rugged plains and mountains alone? I believe they drew from each other as believers in Christ and His Atonement and as they took care of each other's needs, as "sisters in Zion" should.

As sisters we have enough, and even an abundance, to help and lift our fellow sisters. The Lord has put into our hearts the natural desire to lighten the load of our neighbors and sisters. As the hymn says, we are "to cheer and to bless in humanity's name." That is the responsibility we bear as daughters of God in our era or season on the earth. We are under an obligation now, as the Saints were then, to become "as one" by serving each other in an hour of need. How nobly, how faithfully, how bravely we must serve to bring our sisters home.

This is not just a general obligation that has been laid upon us—to have some vague awareness of faceless, nameless, suffering women around the world. As President Dieter F. Uchtdorf has instructed us, we are to "lift where we stand."[1] Think of the needy women in your sphere of influence: The neighbor who is struggling as a single mother to rear her children; the older woman down the street who is widowed and living in solitary loneliness; or the troubled young woman in the ward who is in desperate need of a loving mentor.

As we pass through our own journeys here in life and climb our own Rocky Ridges, as we suffer, and we grow, and we learn, we must look beyond ourselves and help others. This is what Jesus instructed Peter to do—repeating the instruction three times, ensuring that Peter could not misunderstand (see John 21:15–17). I wonder if the Savior might have felt something like this: "Peter, you are falling behind here; I know you love me, but remember that this life experience is not only about you, Peter. If you truly love me, then learn to serve, teach, and lift others even while you are also suffering."

Was this not the very example that Jesus Christ himself was setting for Peter and all of us as well? It is good to remember that before Jesus Christ taught Peter this important lesson, he first fed Peter fish to satisfy his hunger. He served Peter. His message was: "Come, follow me," do as I do, serve as I serve, and love and watch over one another.

Several years ago, a wonderful artist named William Whitaker painted a picture of the Hill sisters. Though it depicts Julia and Emily obviously suffering under the demands of the moment, the noble young women exhibit in this painting a patient and determined feminine strength. They seem to look through time directly at us and say: "Be faithful, dear sisters, in your trials today; be true to the Savior Jesus Christ who prepared the Way for you, who gave His life for you, and who offers you all things if you are faithful. Be grateful for His enabling Atonement, which can cleanse and quicken each individual sister to a higher level of humanity, a higher level of spirituality, and which can glorify us to become even as He is. As we love God with all our heart, might, mind and strength, maybe we can serve and love our sisters as we love ourselves."

This is exactly what Emily penned in her famous poem:

'Tis the office of Angels, conferred upon woman;
and this is a Right that, as woman, we claim;
To do whatsoever is gentle and human;
To cheer and to bless in humanity's name.[2]

She is urging us to be more Christlike individuals—to learn how to pray to God with the best part of us, parting the veil through our obedience, virtue, and the humble words that we send up unto Him daily.

It is interesting how truth is preserved by the faithful for the faithful to find in future years. It is as living breadcrumbs through time that nourish those who are seeking truth. Those who were faithful previously on this earth prepare the way for their brothers and sisters who are coming along later, that these latter-day Saints might be lifted and strengthened in their journey through life. The story of their struggle can also strengthen and encourage sisters across the world today to reach beyond themselves and serve their sisters in need.

If we truly love our God and love and serve our sisters as well, we are destined to become of one heart and therefore to become His. We have the capacity to save others, and they will echo Emily's profound expression of gratitude for those who came to alleviate her need and hopelessness in her poem "Hunger and Cold": "They sought us, and found us, thank God for their pains."[3]

In his inspiring book *To the Rescue,* President Thomas S. Monson issued a call to go out to rescue and save our modern-day, spiritually starving sisters who are languishing on the plains of hopelessness, heartache, and despair.

Throughout my life I have witnessed or participated in many such rescues, and I testify that it is a thrilling, fulfilling, and wonderful work.

My mother suffered from the ravages of Alzheimer's disease for nine years. During that difficult time, my father and my five sisters and I shared the sacred responsibility to care for and assist her. As the time of her passing neared, the seven of us were with her day after day, seeing to her needs. When she finally slipped through the veil, we experienced a tremendous sweetness and exhilaration. We reveled in the closeness we felt as family and as sisters and were profoundly grateful that we had been privileged to work together to serve and to alleviate the suffering of one woman, Dad's sweetheart, and our dear mother.

Not long ago, there was a particularly demanding time in the ward where I lived. Several members of the ward were going through illness, death, and a variety of other discouraging circumstances. Under the direction of our good bishop, the Relief Society sisters participated in an unusually large number of compassionate service projects. Our purpose was to help alleviate the suffering of people who were sick, of families that had lost loved ones, and of sisters who simply needed "a sisterhood" and a listening ear in times of trouble.

The service we provided wasn't unusual; Relief Society sisters all over the world often provide the same kind of loving care. We made simple meals to feed the hungry and homemade greeting cards and quilts for those who needed comfort. We brought a tree and provided simple Christmas presents for a young family whose baby boy had died, and we arranged for homecare nurses from our ward to call on those who were suffering from cancer and other illnesses. We made certain our Relief Society meetings were accessible to all and held them in places that allowed even the sick to attend and participate. We provided the most comfortable chairs in the room to those who were suffering most to ensure that they were a part of the sweet and strengthening messages. We washed clothes and babysat, and the more we served, the greater the love we felt for each other: tall and short, young and old, single and married, widowed and divorced—different, yet exactly the same, and in our service to each other we really felt like sisters. The Spirit was always near during our service for we were on God's compassionate errand.

On another occasion, my husband and I were in Mexico where he was to speak at a stake conference. After an amazing (and long) meeting, I quietly mentioned to my husband that I was hungry. A dear Tzoltzil Indian sister heard me, understood me, and without hesitation handed me her own lunch. I knew that it was a four-to-six-hour truck ride back to her village, and I knew she was as hungry as I was, but I understood her kind gift and took the cornmeal biscuit with both of my hands, kissed her cheek, and thanked her profusely, saying, "Thank you, my dear sister, for giving me your dinner." She beamed, and so did I.

There are so many ways we can love each other! And they need not be difficult. Reach out to each other, for what we do really matters to that one sister. If we take the Holy Ghost as our guide, we will know how and when to serve. Let us not run faster than is needful, but be wise in how we care for one another.

Why was Emily's song preserved for us in our day? As sisters in our noisy, confusing, and almost overwhelming world, I believe we need this message more than ever to survive and even thrive. We are not an island alone, and we need each other to become our best selves. We stand on our own feet and carry our own burdens, but we lift our sisters as we lift ourselves. And most important of all, we know from whence comes our strength as sisters of the latter days: in our Lord and Savior, our Redeemer, Jesus Christ, and in His Atonement.

Other Hymns by
Emily Hill Woodmansee

UPHOLD THE RIGHT, THOUGH FIERCE THE FIGHT

Uphold the right, though fierce the fight, and powerful the foe,
And freedom's friend, her cause defend, nor fear nor favor show.
No coward can be called a man,—No friend will friends betray;
Who will be free, alert must be; and ever watch and pray.

Note how they toil, whose aim is spoil, who plund'ring plots devise;
Yet time will teach that fools o'erreach the mark and lose the prize.
Can justice deign to wrong maintain, whoever wills it so?
Can honor mate with treach'rous hate? Can figs on thistles grow?

Dare to be true, and hopeful, too; be watchful, brave and shrewd.
Weigh ev'ry act; be wise, in fact, to serve the general good.
Nor basely yield, nor quit the field—Important is the fray;
Scorn to recede, there is no need to give our rights away.

Left-handed fraud let those applaud who would by fraud prevail:
In freedom's name, contest their claim, use no such word as fail:
Honor we must each sacred trust, and rightful zeal display;
Our part fulfil, then come what will, high heav'n will clear the way.[14]

RESTING NOW FROM CARE AND SORROW

Resting now from care and sorrow, resting from fatigue and pain;
Faithfully she's fought life's battle—Death to such is endless gain.
God hath gathered home her spirit, God hath taken what He gave;
Friend and sister, sweetly slumber in the quiet, peaceful grave.

All her warfare is accomplished; bid her now a fond adieu;
Brief the parting, glad the meeting, that shall nearest ties renew;
True and tender, self denying, one of Truth's disciples brave—
Let her sleep, she needs to slumber in the quiet, peaceful grave.

Shall we mourn for one who's left us? Yes, our tears we needs must blend;
Love's own off'ring, this, we owe thee, faithful mother, faithful friend;
While we look for consolation unto Him, "The strong to save"—
Friend and sister, sweetly slumber in the quiet, peaceful grave.[15]

COME, SAINTS OF LATTER DAYS

Come, Saints of latter days, unite in cheerful songs;
Come, sing our Father's praise—To whom all praise belongs.
Sing, for the joyful time, by prophets long foretold,
The age of truths sublime our mortal eyes behold.

Look down, ye bards and seers, who sang in ages past,
The Zion of your dreams established is at last.
Zion is famed afar, and more renowned shall be;
Behold! the rising star whose brightness kings shall see.

Let Zion's foes combine to hold her sons in thrall;
Zion by help divine, will triumph over all.
God, in His own good time, will crown the pure and true;
God will be glorified, whate'er the nations do.[16]

WHEN DARK AND DREAR THE SKIES APPEAR

When dark and drear the skies appear,
And doubt and dread would thee enthrall,
Look up, nor fear, the day is near,
And Providence is over all.
From heav'n above, His light and love,
God giveth freely when we call.
Our utmost need is oft decreed,
And Providence is over all.

With jealous zeal God guards our weal,
And lifts our wayward thoughts above,
When storms assail life's bark so frail,
We seek the haven of His love.
And when our eyes transcend the skies,
His gracious purpose is complete.
No more the night distracts our sight—
The clouds are all beneath our feet.

The direst woe that mortals know
Can ne'er the honest heart appall,
Who holds the trust—that God is just,
And Providence is over all.
Should foes increase to mar our peace,
Frustrated all their plans shall fall.
Our utmost need is oft decreed,
And Providence is over all.[17]

OH, BLEST WAS THE DAY WHEN THE PROPHET AND SEER

Oh, blest was the day when the Prophet and Seer,
Who stands at the head of this last dispensation,
Inspired from above by "the Father" of Love,
Form'd the Daughters of Zion's great organization.
Its purpose, indeed, is to comfort and feed
The honest and poor in distress and in need.
Oh, the Daughters of Zion, the friends of the poor,
Should be patterns of faith, hope and charity, pure.

Oh! Daughters of truth, ye have cause to rejoice.
Lo! the key of advancement is placed in your keeping,
To help with your might whatsoever is right,
To gladden their hearts who are weary of weeping,
By commandment divine, Zion's daughters must shine,
And all of the sex, e'en as one, should combine;

For a oneness of action success will ensure,
In resisting the wrongs that 'tis wrong to endure.

O woman! God gave thee the longing to bless:
Thy touch like compassion is warm and caressing,
There's pow'r in thy weakness to soften distress,
To brighten the gloom and the darkness depressing;
And not in the rear, hence, need woman appear;
Her star is ascending, her zenith is near.
Like an angel of mercy, she'll stand in the van,
The joy of the world, and the glory of man.

Oh, be of good cheer, far extending we see,
The rosy-hued dawn like a vision of beauty;
Its glory and light can interpreted be;
Go on in the pathway of love and of duty!
The brave, earnest soul will arrive at its goal.
True heroes are crowned as the ages unroll;
There is blessing in blessing, admit it we must,
And there's honor in helping a cause that is just.[18]

THE DAY OF REDEMPTION, SO NEAR IS AT HAND

The day of redemption, so near is at hand—
We can sing in spite of oppression;
But never to meet e'en a nation's demand,
Will we feign either fear or depression;
The foes of our faith, like the billows, may foam,

"But a rest for the Saints yet remaineth,"
So we'll sing and rejoice in our own mountain home,
That "the Lord God Omnipotent reigneth."

Proscribed for opinion in liberty's land—
Face we bondage, misrule and disaster;
Yet e'en unto death, by the truth may we stand,
And be leal to our Lord and our Master.
But sooner the ocean may quieted be,
And sooner may mortals enchain it,
Than souls can be fettered, whom truth maketh free,
While "the Lord God Omnipotent reigneth."

The heralds of truth yet shall compass the earth
And gather "the wheat" to the garner,
The honest will welcome the tidings of worth,
Undismayed by the wrath of the scorner.
The law of Jehovah we needs must fulfil,
We cannot reject or distain it;
'Tis "the hour of His judgment," and scoffers will feel
That "the Lord God Omnipotent reigneth."

"From the wise and the prudent," the haughty and high
The loftiest truths are oft hidden;
To "the feast of the Bridegroom" whose coming is nigh,
The halt and the humble are bidden.
Thro' obedience, the Lord doth a witness bestow:
Which anyone seeking obtaineth;

And thus do His people assuredly know
That "the Lord God Omnipotent reigneth."

Shall we barter our souls for a nation's applause,
That denies us fair representation?
Are we traitors? Nay, verily, just is our cause,
'Twill survive e'en unjust legislation.
The faith of the Saints shall astonish the world,
And puzzle the wise to explain it;
Hosanna! Hosanna! Truth's flag is unfurled;
And "the Lord God Omnipotent reigneth."[19]

UP! AROUSE THEE, O BEAUTIFUL ZION

Up! arouse thee, O beautiful Zion,
Wake, awake, hear the warder's deep cry,
For the season of slumber hath ended.
And the spoiler is watchful and nigh.
With courage elate and heart to be great,
All deadly encumb'rance cast down,
Gird on for the fight, your armor so bright,
For the prize is a glorious crown.

Up! arouse thee, O beautiful Zion,
Give the mammon-care clouds to the wind,
When the bugle's shrill summons is—Rally!
They are cowards that linger behind.
You've foes to o'ercome in each heart and each home,

Then fixed be your purpose and high.
With God at your head, O feel not dismayed,
But go forward to conquer or die.

Who should shrink from the glorious battle,
With so dazzling a guerdon in view?
If so base as to herd with the traitor,
It is, dastard! not sparkling for you.
Who with nerve strong as steel, and soul that can feel,
Stand firm for the pure and the brave,
Be foremost in right, and trust in God's might—
'Tis such heroes that heaven will save.

Lo! Destruction hangs over the nations,
Tho' not seen by the unholy throng;
And death will be heard in the echoes
Of the gathering, ominous storm!
Then arouse, thee, O beautiful Zion,
Wake, awake, 'tis the warder's deep cry,
For the season of slumber is ended,
And the spoiler is watchful and nigh! [20]

Notes

CHAPTER ONE: "AS SISTERS IN ZION"

Epigraph: Emily Hill Woodmansee in Crocheron, *Representative Women of Deseret*, 83.

1. Ibid., 82.
2. Ibid., 83.
3. Ibid., 84.
4. Ibid., 83.
5. Ibid., 84.
6. Ibid., 85.
7. Ibid., 84.
8. Ibid., 85.
9. Woodmansee, "Is My Father Yet Alive?" in Abegg, *Poetry of Emily Woodmansee*, 197.
10. Ibid.
11. Ibid.
12. Woodmansee, "My Mother," in Abegg, *Poetry of Emily Woodmansee*, 277.
13. Woodmansee in Crocheron, *Representative Women of Deseret*, 85.
14. "A Compilation of General Voyage Notes" in "Thornton: Liverpool to New York."
15. Lyman, *The Willie Handcart Company*, 14.
16. "A Compilation of General Voyage Notes" in "Thornton: Liverpool to New York."
17. "Letter from James G. Willie—June 11, 1856," in "Thornton: Liverpool to New York."
18. Willie, "Synopsis."

19. Ibid.
20. Ibid.
21. Ibid.
22. Woodmansee in Crocheron, *Representative Women of Deseret,* 86.

CHAPTER TWO: "WE'LL ALL WORK TOGETHER"

Epigraph: James G. Willie in Smith, "Faithful Stewards."

1. Thorne, et al., "Isaac Campkin and Martha Webb History."
2. Ririe, "Martha Webb Campkin Young."
3. Teresa Young Grover, letter to author, June 26, 2004.
4. William Woodward in Smith, "Faithful Stewards."
5. Thorne, et al, "Isaac Campkin and Martha Webb History."
6. William Woodward in Olsen, *Price We Paid,* 71.
7. Willie in Smith, "Faithful Stewards."
8. Willie, "Synopsis," 11.
9. Woodmansee in Crocheron, *Representative Women of Deseret,* 86.
10. Willie, "Synopsis," 10.

CHAPTER THREE: "THE BLESSINGS OF GOD ON OUR LABORS WE'LL SEEK"

Epigraph: Woodmansee, "Hunger and Cold," in Abegg, *Poetry of Emily Woodmansee,* 168.

1. Chislett, "Narrative."
2. Willie, "Synopsis," 11.
3. "Latest News from the Plains."
4. Willie, "Synopsis," 11.
5. William Woodward in Smith, "Faithful Stewards."
6. Woodmansee in Crocheron, *Representative Women of Deseret,* 86.
7. Olsen, *Price We Paid,* 132–33.
8. Woodmansee, "Hunger and Cold," in Abegg, *Poetry of Emily Woodmansee,* 168–70.

CHAPTER FOUR: "WITH EARNEST ENDEAVOR"

Epigraph: Levi Savage in Olsen, *Price We Paid,* 152.

1. Chislett, "Narrative."
2. Ibid.
3. Chislett in Olsen, *Price We Paid,* 150.

4. Savage in Olsen, *Price We Paid,* 152.

5. Erdman, *Israel Ivins,* 12.

CHAPTER FIVE: "THE ERRAND OF ANGELS"

Epigraph: Francis Webster in Olsen, *Price We Paid,* 424.

1. Young, in *Journal of Discourses,* 4:89, 91; emphasis added.

2. Ibid., 91.

3. Webster in Olsen, *Price We Paid,* 423–24.

CHAPTER SIX: "OH, NAUGHT BUT THE SPIRIT'S DIVINEST TUITION"

Epigraph: Woodmansee, "My Sister," in Abegg, *Poetry of Emily Woodmansee,* 281.

1. Ririe, "Life Story of Martha Webb Campkin Young."

2. Allphin, *Tell My Story, Too,* 53.

3. Patriarchal blessing of Julia Hill Ivins, given October 31, 1870, St. George, Utah. Copy in possession of author.

4. Woodmansee, "My Sister," in Abegg, *Poetry of Emily Woodmansee,* 281–83.

5. William G. Mills, "Arise, O Glorious Zion," in *Hymns* (1985), no. 40.

6. "Alexandrina Bray."

7. Woodmansee in Crocheron, *Representative Women of Deseret,* 86–87.

8. Ibid., 86.

9. Ibid., 87.

10. Whitney, *History of Utah,* 594.

11. Ibid.

12. Woodmansee, "Song of the Sisters of the Female Relief Society," in Abegg, *Poetry of Emily Woodmansee,* 405.

13. Woodmansee in Crocheron, *Representative Women of Deseret,* 85.

CHAPTER SEVEN: "TO CHEER AND TO BLESS IN HUMANITY'S NAME"

Epigraph: Woodmansee, "Song of the Sisters of the Female Relief Society," in Abegg, *Poetry of Emily Woodmansee,* 405.

1. Dieter F. Uchtdorf, "Lift Where You Stand," *Ensign,* November 2008, 53.

2. Woodmansee, "Song of the Sisters," *Poetry of Emily Woodmansee,* 405.

3. Woodmansee, "Hunger and Cold," *Poetry of Emily Woodmansee,* 168.

Notes

Other Hymns by Emily Hill Woodmansee

1. Woodmansee, "Uphold the Right, though Fierce the Fight," in *Latter-day Saint Hymns* (1927), no. 93.
2. Ibid., "Resting Now from Care and Sorrow," *Hymns* (1927), no. 201.
3. Ibid., "Come, Saints of Latter Days," *Hymns* (1927), no. 208.
4. Ibid., "When Dark and Drear the Skies Appear," *Hymns* (1927), no. 210.
5. Ibid., "Oh, Blest Was the Day When the Prophet and Seer," *Hymns* (1927), no. 377.
6. Ibid., "The Day of Redemption, So Near Is at Hand," *Hymns* (1927), no. 378.
7. Ibid., "Up! Arouse Thee, O Beautiful Zion," *Hymns* (1927), no. 390 and no. 413.

Sources Consulted

Great appreciation is extended to Janice Kapp Perry for her initial research into this story and also to Robert and Colleen Bentley for sharing their family history collection.

BOOKS

Abegg, Myrlon Bentley. *The Poetry of Emily Hill Woodmansee.* Published privately, 1986.

Allphin, Jolene S. *Tell My Story, Too.* Published privately, 2001.

Crocheron, Augusta Joyce, comp. *Representative Women of Deseret.* Salt Lake City: J. C. Graham & Co., 1884.

Erdman, Kimball Stewart. *Israel Ivins: A Biography.* Published privately, 1969.

Garner, Ceytru B., comp. *Richard Ivins Bentley: His Family and Some Life Experiences.* Published privately, 2008.

Hymns of The Church of Jesus Christ of Latter-day Saints. Salt Lake City: The Church of Jesus Christ of Latter-day Saints, 1985.

Journal of Discourses. 26 vols. London: Latter-day Saints' Book Depot, 1854–86.

Latter-day Saint Hymns. Salt Lake City: Deseret Book, 1927.

Lyman, Paul D. *The Willie Handcart Company: Their Day-by-Day Experiences, Including Trail Maps and Driving Directions.* Provo, UT: BYU Studies, 2006.

Olsen, Andrew D. *The Price We Paid: The Extraordinary Story of the Willie & Martin Handcart Pioneers.* Salt Lake City: Deseret Book, 2006.

Whitney, Orson F. *History of Utah.* 4 vols. Salt Lake City: George Q. Cannon & Sons, 1904.

Sources Consulted

PERIODICALS

Uchtdorf, Dieter F. "Lift Where You Stand." *Ensign,* November 2008, 53–55.

JOURNALS

Journal History of The Church of Jesus Christ of Latter-day Saints. November 9–19, 1856. Church History Library, Salt Lake City, Utah.

"Latest News from the Plains." *The Mormon,* November 15, 1856, 3. In Journal History of The Church of Jesus Christ of Latter-day Saints. Church History Library, Salt Lake City, Utah.

Willie, James G. "Synopsis of the 4th Handcart Company's Trip from Liverpool, England, to Great Salt Lake City in the Spring, Summer and Autumn of 1856." November 9, 1856. In Journal History of The Church of Jesus Christ of Latter-day Saints. Church History Library, Salt Lake City, Utah.

WEBSITES

"Alexandrina Bray." Barbarowa Genealogy. http://brooklyncentre.com/trees/getperson. php?personID=I16374&tree=Brainard.

Chislett, John. "Narrative." In Mormon Pioneer Overland Travel, 1847–1868. http:// lds.org/churchhistory/library/source/1,18016,4976–86169,00.html.

Perry, Janice Kapp. "As Sisters in Zion—Born a Century Apart." Lost Hymns Project. http://www.losthymnsproject.com/Hymnastics_101/as_sisters_in_zion.htm.

Ririe, David. "Life Story of Martha Webb Campkin Young." Ririe.org: The Online Resource for the James E. Ririe Family. http://www.ririe.org/history/documents/ martha_webb_campkin_story.asp.

Smith, Marilyn Austin. "Faithful Stewards—The Life of James Gray Willie and Elizabeth Ann Pettit." In Mormon Pioneer Overland Travel, 1847–1868. http:// lds.org/churchhistory/library/source/1,18016,4976–7462,00.html.

Thorne, Ida Young, Martha A. Merrell, and Clarice Y. Whitesides, edited by Keith Young. "Isaac Campkin and Martha Webb History." Youngzones.org. http://www. youngzones.org/~nkyoung/IsaacCampkinHistory.html.

"Thornton: Liverpool to New York." Mormon Migration. Brigham Young University. http://lib.byu.edu/mormonmigration/voyage.php?id=343.